PIANO / VOCAL / GUITAR

# TOP HITS OF 2012

ISBN 978-1-4768-1764-4

HAL•LEONARD®
CORPORATION
7777 W. BLUEMOUND RD. P.O. BOX 13819 MILWAUKEE, WI 53213

Visit Hal Leonard Online at
www.halleonard.com

# CONTENTS

# BOYFRIEND

Words and Music by JUSTIN BIEBER,
MAT MUSTO, MIKE POSNER
and MASON LEVY

**Moderate Hip-Hop groove**

*\* Recorded a half step lower.*

# DRIVE BY

Words and Music by PAT MONAHAN,
ESPEN LIND and AMUND BJORKLAND

**Moderately fast**

On the oth-er side of a street I knew stood a girl that looked like you.
On the up-side of a down-ward spi-ral, my __ love for you went vi-ral,

I guess that's dé-jà vu, but I thought, "This can't be true," _ 'cause
and I loved you ev-'ry mile _____ you drove a-way.

you moved to West L. A. or New York or San-ta Fe, ___ or
But now here you are a-gain, so let's skip the "how you been" _ and

To Coda ⊕

Oh, I swear to you I'll be there for you. This is not a drive

by - y - y - y - y.

by - y - y - y - y.

Please be - lieve that when I leave

there's noth - ing up my sleeve but love for you,

# GLAD YOU CAME

Words and Music by STEVE MAC,
WAYNE HECTOR and EDWARD DREWETT

**Electro Pop**

The sun goes down, the stars come __ out and all that

counts is here and __ now. My u - ni - verse will nev - er be the

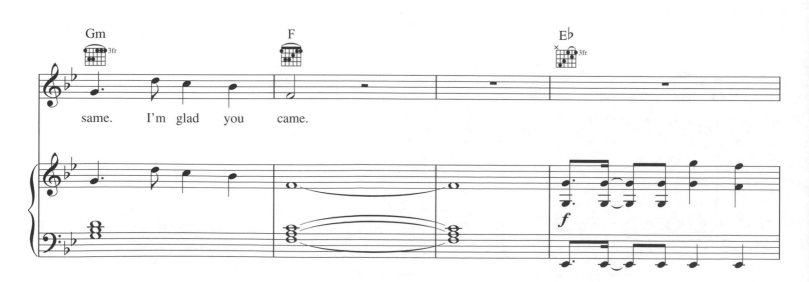

same. I'm glad you came.

18

# GOOD GIRL

Words and Music by CHRIS DeSTEFANO,
ASHLEY GORLEY and CARRIE UNDERWOOD

Hey, good girl, with your
good girl, you got a

head in the clouds, __ I bet you I can tell you what you're think-in' a - bout. You see a
heart __ of gold, __ you want a white __ wed-ding and a hand you can hold. __ Just like you

# HOME

Words and Music by GREG HOLDEN
and DREW PEARSON

# THE ONE THAT GOT AWAY

Words and Music by KATY PERRY,
MAX MARTIN and LUKASZ GOTTWALD

# SET FIRE TO THE RAIN

Words and Music by ADELE ADKINS
and FRASER SMITH

# OURS

Words and Music by
TAYLOR SWIFT

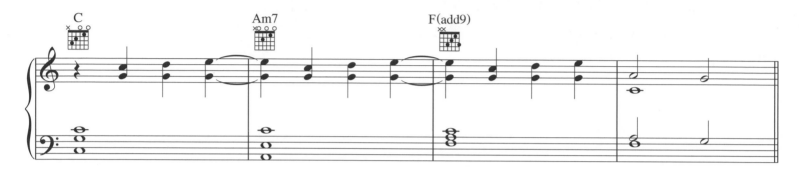

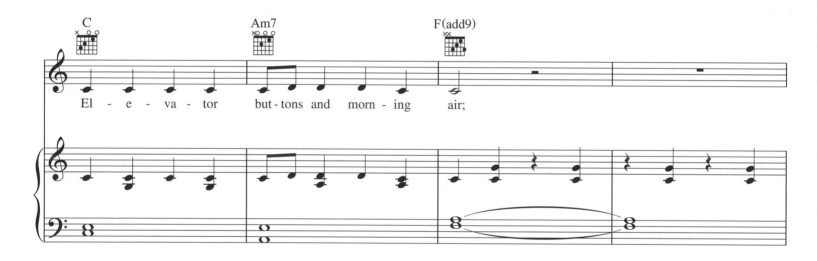

El - e - va - tor but - tons and morn - ing air;

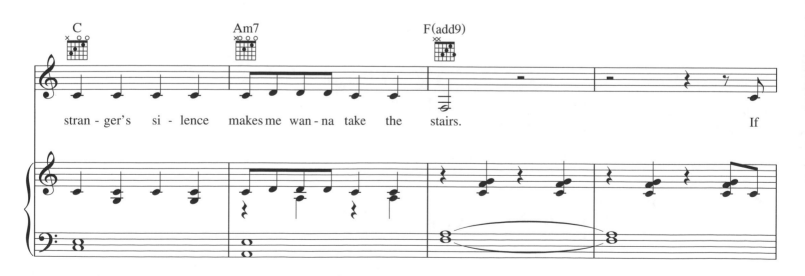

stran - ger's si - lence makes me wan - na take the stairs.          If

You

ours.

And it's not theirs to spec - u - late ___ if it's wrong. And

# PAYPHONE

Words and Music by ADAM LEVINE,
BENJAMIN LEVIN, AMMAR MALIK,
JOHAN SCHUSTER, DANIEL OMELIO
and WIZ KHALIFA

**Moderately fast**

*I'm at a pay - phone try - in' to call___ home. All of my change___ I spent___ on you.___ Where have the times___ gone? Ba - by, it's all___ wrong. Where are the plans___ we made___ for two?___ Yeah, I,*

\* *Recorded a half step higher.*

**D.S. al Coda**

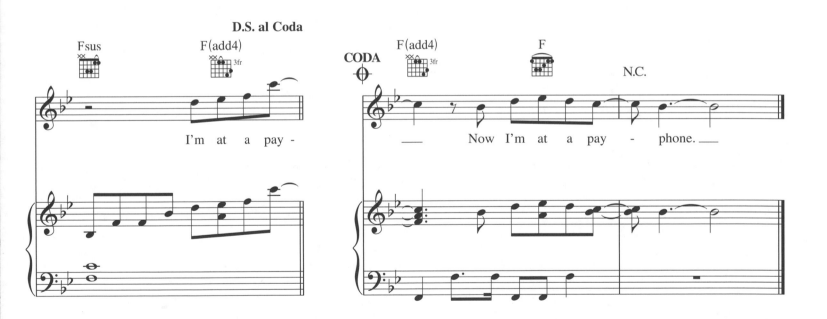

I'm at a pay -

**CODA** Now I'm at a pay - phone. __

*Rap Lyrics*

Man, f\*\*k that sh\*\*. I'll be out spending all this money while you're sittin' 'round
Wondering why it wasn't you who came up from nothin'. Made it from the bottom. Now when you see me I'm stuntin'.
And all of my cars start with a push of a button, tellin' me the chances I blew up, or whatever you call it.
Switched the number to my phone so you never could call it. Don't need my name; on my shirt you can tell it, I'm ballin'.

Swish. What a shame, coulda got picked. Had a really good game but you missed your last
Shot, so you talk about who you see at the top, or what you coulda saw, but sad to say, you saw before.
Phantom pull up, valet open doors. Wished I'd go away; got what you was lookin' for.
Now it's me who they want, so you can go and take that little piece of sh\*\* wit' ya.

# RUMOUR HAS IT

Words and Music by ADELE ADKINS
and RYAN TEDDER

**With energy and soul**

# STRONGER
## (What Doesn't Kill You)

Words and Music by GREG KURSTIN,
JORGEN ELOFSSON, DAVID GAMSON
and ALEXANDRA TAMPOSI

# WHERE HAVE YOU BEEN

Words and Music by CALVIN HARRIS,
ESTHER DEAN, LUKASZ GOTTWALD,
GEOFF MACK and HENRY WALTER

**Moderate Dance groove**

Where have you been? _____ 'Cause I nev-er see\_\_ you out. \_\_

Are you hid-in' from me _____

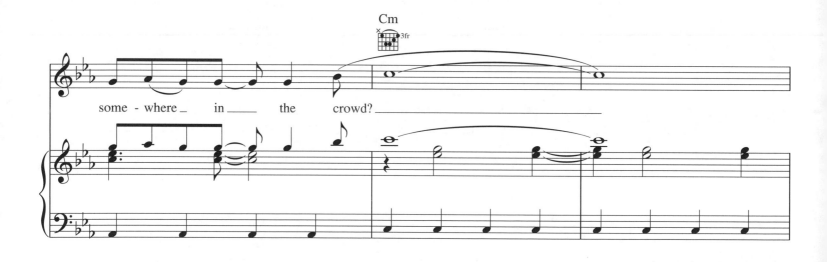

some-where \_ in \_\_ the crowd? _____

Yeah, yeah, yeah, yeah, yeah, yeah. Yeah, yeah,

# WHAT MAKES YOU BEAUTIFUL

Words and Music by SAVAN KOTECHA,
RAMI YACOUB and CARL FALK

**Moderate Pop**

You're in - se - cure,      don't know what   for.      You're turn - in'
mon,      you got it   wrong.      To prove I'm

heads  when you walk through the   do - o - or.    Don't need make - up      to cov - er
right,  I put it in a   so - o - ong.    I don't know why      you're be - ing